Praise for *M*

"A rare and vibrant exploration[...]p[...]y when it comes to America's history and traditions, *Made to Explode* is a courageous interrogation of self, culture, and how we are made. Both unflinching and tender, [Sandra] Beasley's smart and radiant poems glow with a historian's exactitude and a poet's lyrical heart."

—Ada Limón, United States poet laureate and author of *The Carrying*

"*Made to Explode* makes no attempt whatsoever to fight shy of dazzling and rafter-rattling detonation. Here the poet, known for her smooth mastery of craft and lyric, examines a life lived in and around the capital of her fractured and restless country. She aims unerringly at the contradictions of lush, picture-book days in Virginia, and later DC, with its paradoxes, its stern testaments, its stone institutions. In the process, she redefines her own root. There is unwavering insight in these poems. There is tenderness and personal revelation. There is everything we waited for."

—Patricia Smith, author of *Incendiary Art*

"I know I am reading a Sandra Beasley poem when precision and music are driven by emotive, passionate force. . . . But what I most recommend, and what I am most compelled by in these pages is their engagement with American history. 'Ruth Bader Ginsburg sits in the nineteenth row of my heart,' writes Beasley in what, in the end, becomes a book of reckoning. Beasley questions the late empire, yes, but perhaps more importantly, more honestly: she questions herself. Which is why, I think, this is a most beautiful book: you will find virtuoso music, and necessary clarity."

—Ilya Kaminsky, author of *Deaf Republic*

"Beasley greets the world in this collection with curiosity and intelligence and makes a space for the important reckoning of our universal American heritages."

—Amanda Auchter, *Indianapolis Review*

"A litany of sensual pleasures and careful self-reckoning. . . . Beasley uses her trademark humor and wit to explore the heavier parts of personal and national identity in this energetic and varied outing." —*Publishers Weekly*

"[Beasley's] exploration of the construct and historical responsibility of a white woman in today's American culture is both nuanced and surreal. . . . *Made to Explode* is a complex book, written with exquisite craft. It tackles a series of subjects not easy to talk about in polite company, shining a light on an intersection where we, the reader, may choose a cab, to figure out which way to leave—or maybe we like it here, too."—Danelle Lejeune, *Wraparound South*

Made to Explode

Made to Explode

Poems

SANDRA BEASLEY

100

W. W. NORTON & COMPANY
Celebrating a Century of Independent Publishing

For information about permission to reproduce selections from this book,
write to Permissions, W. W. Norton & Company, Inc.,
500 Fifth Avenue, New York, NY 10110

For information about special discounts for bulk purchases, please contact
W. W. Norton Special Sales at specialsales@wwnorton.com or 800-233-4830

Manufacturing by LSC Harrisonburg

Library of Congress Cataloging-in-Publication Data

Names: Beasley, Sandra, author.
Title: Made to explode : poems / Sandra Beasley.
Description: First Edition. | New York, NY : W. W. Norton & Company, [2021]
Identifiers: LCCN 2020036689 | ISBN 9780393531602 (hardcover) |
ISBN 9780393531619 (epub)
Subjects: LCGFT: Poetry.
Classification: LCC PS3602.E2558 M33 2021 | DDC 811/.6—dc23
LC record available at https://lccn.loc.gov/2020036689

ISBN 978-1-324-03600-5 pbk.

W. W. Norton & Company, Inc., 500 Fifth Avenue, New York, N.Y. 10110
www.wwnorton.com

W. W. Norton & Company Ltd., 15 Carlisle Street, London W1D 3BS

1 2 3 4 5 6 7 8 9 0

For the grandmothers

Contents

*   *   *

* * *

Made to Explode

HEIRLOOM

Lo, twelve children born to a woman named Thankful
in Nampa, by the border between Oregon
and Idaho, or as it will be remembered: Ore-Ida.
Lo, two of her sons drive to Miami
not knowing if their plan will work.
Lo, what were once waste scraps fed to the cows
now repackaged—the fry shavings sliced, spiced, and oiled.
Lo, a chef at the Fountainebleau takes the bribe.
Lo, Tater Tots are dished onto the tables
of the 1954 National Potato Convention and soon,
enshrined in the freezers of America. Three decades later,
the golden age of my childhood is a foil-lined tray
plattered with Ore-Ida product, maybe salt, maybe
nothing but hot anticipation of my fingertips.
Lo, my mother is a great cook and Lo,
my grandmother is a terrible one, but on tinfoil plains
they are equal. I need you to understand
why my father will never enjoy an heirloom tomato
glistening, layered in basil. Put away your Brandywines,
your Cherokee Purples, your Green Zebras.
Lo, as with spinach, as with olives, he tastes only
the claustrophobia his mother unleashed from cans

to feed four children on a budget. We talk little of this.
Lo, what is cooked to mush.
Lo, what is peppered to ash. Lo, the flavor
rendered as morning chore—that this, too, is a form of love.

ELEPHANT

On the Route 7 strip,
next to the office supply store,
next to the pool supply store,
next to the Tower Records,
next to the T.J. Maxx,
the Ranger Surplus lurked

where I shopped only
at the edges: iron-on patches,
all-weather lighters,
vintage plate pin-ups,
never venturing into the groin
of camouflage and camping gear,

until I began buying weapons
including a mace, a chained flail,
several throwing stars, and the book
Contemporary Surveillance Techniques,
with its cover art showing a man
crouched in a stereo speaker,

all gifts for my father,
because what do you get the man
who has everything—and by *everything*
I mean a large-caliber shell casing
upright and decorative
in the living room, where you might

expect a potted ficus to be—
and these, too,
were the years he gave me
T-shirt after T-shirt, souvenirs
of every posting and deployment,
including the one that said

Hard Rock Cafe Baghdad—
Closed—Kuwait, Now Reopening—
T-shirts that fit poorly
over my new breasts, boxy,
unflattering, and so I shut them
away in drawers again

and again, each of us
trying to say to the other
I see you,
the way a blindfolded man
takes the tail into his hands, believing
from this he can see the elephant.

LONG JOHN SILVER'S

Once again at the Long John Silver's of 1988
the rope-slung walkway seems to sway under my feet
as I look up at the Cape Cod with its steepled roof,
trimmed in yellow, and lean my whole weight
to the wrought-iron sword that serves as a door handle.
At the counter, I order a fish fillet
served in a folded paper Treasure Chest with
a handful of fries to hide the Secret Compartment;
hold the hush puppies, corn cob on the side.
I carry the blue plastic tray with care to a booth
paneled in the mahogany of an officer's quarters,
then sit on a bench vinyled like a nautical flag.
The batter is always fluffy with club soda
and here, no one has died yet.
My teeth cut a smile into the Icelandic cod,
and perhaps I will go back to order a chicken plank
or a tray of crunchies swept from fryer's belly,
which they will give me for free.
When I look back on all that I've done, I want
to be the person stubborn enough to found a chain
of Seafood Shoppes in Lexington, Kentucky,

five hundred miles from any ocean,
named for a character in a Scottish novel.
I want to admit I'm doubled over and howling,
yet reach up to ring the Captain's Bell on my way out.

THE CONVERSATION

Fireflies, Col. Glenn calls them—
banging the capsule's wall to prove
their movement. This
will be the gesture Hollywood
claims as history—how space
dazzles even the seasoned airman,

maddens like Titania's touch.
The movie version sees
what he sees: Florida yawn, Delta yawp,
a sunrise inside every hour,
lightning over the Indian Ocean.
Yet the operatic soundtrack, paced

in gilded silence, is not what he hears.
Wonder-ese is not the language
he speaks. For this,
we turn to the transcript. Pilot
to Cap Com; Cap Com to Pilot.
This is Friendship 7, going to manual.

Ah, Roger, Friendship 7.
Pilot, Texas Cap Com, Cape Canaveral.
Cap Coms chiming in from Canary,

Canton, Hawaii, Zanzibar, India,
Woomera: every visual check
on the gyros, inverter temp,

every correction to pitch and yaw,
fuel, oxygen, *Ah, Roger, Ah, Over.*
Say again your instructions please.
Over. Do you read? *Stand by.*
You can be honest. This
is *Godspeed*-less, workaday chatter.

But in these pages
my grandfather lives forever—
a Navy captain charged
with Glenn's vitals, stretching
his stethoscope across 162 miles
and eighteen tracking stations.

I hear him in each pressure check.
I see him biting his lip,
leaning toward a bank of dials
while the retropackage breaks, burns.
No one knows if the heat shield
will hold. Captain Pruett

goes unnamed. This
is how history claims us:
not in the gesture of one but
in the conversation of many,
the talk that gets the job done.
We climb into the syrup-can capsule

to circle the Earth three times.
The miraculous swarm,
we will realize,
is condensation. The light
blinks at us,
flake and ice of our own breath.

WINTZELL'S OYSTER HOUSE

Before six seats and a trough of oysters,
before J. Oliver slathers the wall in homespun,
Charles W. Peters sells squash here, and canned beans;
he sells bed frames & dressers & side tables;
insurance against rising waters;
he sells whatever will send nine daughters and sons
through college. In 1891, a Black man
can build two stories of clapboard for $2,000,
can aspire to his own furniture company,
can preside over the Mutual Aid Association,
can march with 4,000 men and four brass bands
under the Emancipation League's auspices.
He builds two blocks from the Creole Fire Station,
which keeps fast horses, racetrack rejects,
because the first fire-truck to arrive on the scene
is the only one whose men get paid.
Fifty-some years later, a merchant marine
offered West Indies by way of Mobile:
crab lumped, layered in fine-chopped onion
& the kiss of Wesson oil,
& the slap of iced water & how God

means for salad to be served, on a saltine.
We chow down in the last all-wood joint on Dauphin.
The secret is in the cider vinegar, how
a hundred jaws of minor angels macerate the haul.

NOSTALGIA

An adult shad has 1,300 bones,
but that's not why I always order it:
I remember fingers of white flesh, flaky-fried,
or a sac of red roe slapped into a pan
with a pat of butter,
and I think of camping by the James River,
how the sky yawned and hollered.
I once loved a band named Emmet Swimming.
I got lost in a crowd of teenagers
inscribing each other's yearbooks in blue Bic ink,
working hard for a house with fake wood trim,
singing that it's a long way down,
wondering how long it'd been since I'd been good.
We were sweat-sweet and dancing.
We paid what we could afford at the door.
Two decades later, I read the band named themselves
for Emmett Till.
The lead singer says the name means
a fourteen-year-old should be swimming in the river,
not dying in it.
They spelled his name wrong and,
once they realized that,
they kept spelling his name wrong.
I've got 1,290 pin bones to go.

WE GOT AN A—

We your friends.
We the Virginians.
We the northern Virginians.
We the eleventh grade.
We the choir parties.
We the Madonna sing-alongs.
We the third-period U.S. History.
We the antebellum economies.
We the Sunday, the Doritos and Jolt.
We the directors.
We the script.
We the farmers.
We the farmers' wives.
You, we decide,
should play the cotton picker.
You who vogues best of any of us.
You stand in the closet
with a Tylenol bottle, teasing
puffs of white from its open mouth.
We your friends.
We the northern Virginians.

We the Virginians.
We the video camera, waiting.
We who swear This Will Be Hilarious.
The door opens. The skit begins.

MONTICELLO PEACHES

Jefferson planted over a thousand trees
in the South Orchard—eighteen varieties of apple,
six apricot, four nectarine,
and thirty-eight types of peach.
Lemon Cling. Heath Cling. Indian Blood Cling.
Vaga Loggia. Breast of Venus,
which Jefferson accounted for as the "teat peach"—
interlopers mistaken as indigenous.
Each cleft globe was a luxury,
yet so abundant they were sliced, chipped,
boiled, brandied, fried, sun-dried,
and extras fed to the hogs.

> *My first wish is that the labourers*
> *may be well treated,*
> the Master wrote.
> He created a system for tipping.
> Once, James Hemings was whipped
> three times over before the sun had set
> behind Brown's Mountain.

When Jefferson traveled to Paris
in 1784, he took Sally and her brother—
James, who learned the language,

who trained at pasta and pastry,
paid four dollars per month to serve
as chef de cuisine to the Minister to France.
James, who had to be coaxed to leave
a country where, in 1789,
slavery had been abolished.

> *I hereby do promise & declare*
> *until he shall have taught such person*
> *as I shall place under him for that purpose*
> *to be a good cook, this previous condition*
> *being performed,*
> *he shall thereupon be made free . . .*
> "For that purpose": their brother, Robert.

In 1796, James was freed.
In 1801, James killed himself.
In 1802, Robert debuted macaroni pie
on the menu for Jefferson's state dinner.
In 1824, a recipe layering pasta, cheese, and butter
appears in *The Virginia Housewife: Or, Methodical Cook*,
alongside Mrs. Mary Randolph's marmalade
that specifies a pound of West Indies sugar
to two pounds of peaches—"yellow ones

make the prettiest"—and a hard chop
until flesh gives away to transparent pulp,
chilled to a jelly.

> If one was accused of stealing or eating
> beyond one's share
> the grill was secured
> over the mouth.
> This was considered the kind muzzle.
> The unkind one settled an iron bit
> over the tongue.

The groundskeepers knew we'd come
with our wreath to lay at Jefferson's grave,
walking Monticello's grass at misted dawn,
half-drunk and laughing.
We came every year.
There are two types of peaches:
one to which the stone clings,
shredding to wet threads,
and another allowed to lift clean.

> "Freestone," they call those peaches—
> that most popular variety, the White Lady.

TOPSY TURVY

A style of doll original to plantation culture
and mass-manufactured well into the twentieth century,
later reworked to feature fairy-tale characters.

Lovable Topsy, charming Eva,
the adaptable pattern:

Little Red Riding Hood
with stitch-mouth, her big eyes,

her gingham apron. Flip her,
reverse her skirts—

one face covered, another bared—
now she's Grandmother

with perched glasses, mob cap.
Yank and tuck the elastic,

fussing the cap back and down
to cover Grandma's face,

and where her silvering bun
might be, he waits:

Turn me up / And turn me back,
I once was white / And now am black.

What good is a tale,
I was taught,

without the Big Bad Wolf?
His pointed ears, his fangs,

his expanse of charcoal
and slavering pup-tongue.

Little flip-figure, little relic.
Give him a howl.

In the toy basket one day
& one day & one day & one day

& *Where did this come from?*
& then the doll was gone.

MY WHITENESSES

Whiteness as my body's
spent currency:
hair that holds no melanin,
which I pluck out;
an overlong fingernail
that I tear away;
what once blistered,
collapsed flat to my heel.
And what then?
Skin picked, flicked
under my bed—
strands dropped to tile—
the keratin crescents folded,
tucked in couch-crevice.
My performative strip
of self, still
trashing up the place.
Down by Richmond,
how you pronounce a thing
sets stake in the land.
Do you elaborate
a tribe's *Pow-hite*?
Or does 300 years

of muscle memory
guide the tongue?
Po' white Creek.
Po' white Parkway.
One man uses *cracker*
as absolution,
as proof of brotherhood,
while another uses *cracker*
because someone,
three great-grands ago,
cracked a whip.
Virginia, my ghosts
need gathering.
Come to the table
and sit, goddammit. Sit.

BLACK DEATH SPECTACLE

A Golden Shovel
after Gwendolyn Brooks,
"The Last Quatrain of the Ballad of Emmett Till."

A man asks those viewing *Open Casket* what comes after
their shock, when from the
safe distance of cocktails the boy's murder
becomes a matter of palette, of line and stroke, after
someone fumbles their way through the
—*drowned? Was he drowned?* Wasn't the Chicago burial
a kind of show, they say, curated by Emmett's
mother? The painter says, *And I, too, am a mother.*

Our tools seduce. Ask what the shovel is
burying. Know that the paintbrush sees only a
canvas: *Make it yours. Make it pretty.*

Carolyn Bryant is here and shit-faced
again and muttering that she couldn't do a damn thing
to stop them, bacon burned, wheels off the
wagon, that if her husband had heard even a tint
of recanting he'd have slapped her silly. Of
course she's here— moth pulled
to the flame, one kid jealous of another's taffy.
Now that a white woman's hands are all over this, she
wants in. Carolyn paces, paces, sits.

Ask the poet what gets colored in.
Ask the poet what gets colored in a
red
room.
Ask the poet who sits in a red room, drinking.

Most oil painters will not use pure black.
They build their black instead, from shades of coffee
and navy. When she
leans toward the painting she almost kisses
the tacky surface. *There.* She adjusts the spot-lamp, her
skin catching the glow off what has been killed.

Emmett Till is a fourteen-year-old boy,
quick to laugh and
to help his mother with the laundry, and she
offers driving lessons if they go to Omaha. But he is
determined to be Mississippi-bound. Does he say sorry?
Does he promise, *next time?* Before the chaos,
he tucks a pack of bubblegum in
his pocket. She brings him home to the windy
city so thousands can file by in their best church grays.

At the Biennial, the man's T-shirt challenges those passing through.
BLACK DEATH SPECTACLE. They murmur over the bloom of a
wound, seeing red without seeing red.
Question the shovel, he says, that'd till this prairie.

WEAK OCEAN

The quake was born in Mineral, Virginia, and traveled north with a magnitude of 5.8. Cracks appeared in the Washington Monument. The cathedral lost two pinnacles. To explain the damage, seismologists will announce that we sit on only the thinnest layer of silts—"weak ocean sediments"—and beneath that, crystalline rock whose shaking energy creates an echo chamber of the soft mud. I drive to her house, ninety miles north of Mineral, and park where she used to grow snapdragons. I wait on the porch where geraniums stood sentry, nodding their incomplete heads. We walk the house together, straightening paintings. My job is to move dishtowels from the stove's burners and check for mold in the fridge. She worries about getting things in order for "the girls." No one knows who "the girls" are. What about the china? Her crystal flutes? The dining room is dusty, samovar hunkering in a corner. We peer through the cabinet's leaded panes at teacups and gilded saucers, champagne coupes. Only when I open the door do they give in to gravity—stacks of porcelain that sag and swing, fractures vertebral, glass popping. She laughs, a kindness or symptom. Someone always lets the earthquake out.

THE SNIPER DANCE

We needed bacon and bread, so we went to Magruder's. We needed gas, so we stopped at Exxon. Kids got on the school bus. We watched for a white Chevy Astro. *Dear Policeman*, the tarot card said, *I am God.* The woman shot in the parking lot at Seven Corners was an FBI analyst, the newspapers would tell us later. She'd studied mathematics. She'd once been held at machete point in Guatemala City. She coached skiing in Stuttgart and tennis in Okinawa. While teaching in Belgium, her house burned. She raised two children. Her chest was marked by a double mastectomy, still healing. She phoned her father and promised, *We're just going out to Home Depot and that's it.* Later, her husband remembered wet flicking the side of his face. The snipers took Interstate 66 and got locked in traffic, a gaze away from an off-duty officer. But they drove a Chevrolet Caprice, a dark blue sedan, and we were all looking for an Astro. Witnesses gave partial plates for a light-colored van. Our dance was discernible only in transition: casual gait; casual gait; casual gait; then the head ducked, swerve to the left, a bag hitched—to throw off his aim, wherever the sniper might be waiting.

KISS ME

Ruth Bader Ginsburg sits in the nineteenth row of my heart
while onstage, a woman has been conscribed to the shape of a
shrew. The actress has forty-carat eyes, an aquiline nose; her
shoulders slight, her waist small enough. She is spanked over
our hero's knee. Everyone is laughing except the conductor,
who must steady his baton, and the house manager, who has
seen it before, and the actors directed instead to be aghast,
agape, gawking, agog, whatever Cole Porter rhymes with
dismayed, and Ginsburg, who adjusts the pearl clipped to her
ear. She curls the program in her lap. This is tiring, attending
theaters of the heart. She doesn't relish it as Sandra Day
O'Connor did, sipping prosecco at the intermission of *Porgy
& Bess*. The gangsters soft-shoe, reminding us to brush up
on our Shakespeare. The actress sings "I Am Ashamed That
Women Are So Simple." Soon, Kate will be tamed. That's how
we know the ending is happy.

JEFFERSON, MIDNIGHT

In another version of this story, he is a naturalist who dabbled in politics. He reinvented the plow. He joined the American Philosophical Society's Bone Committee and, while trying to prove the great Western lion, gave us our first giant sloth. He shipped a rotting moose to France to demonstrate the greatness of our mammals. He is a father of paleontology who didn't believe extinction was part of God's plan. He asked Lewis and Clark, should they encounter the mammoth, to capture one. For months his sea wall has been sinking, the Potomac's mud flats sucking at support timbers. In 1918 and for six summers after, the Tidal Basin was chlorinated so this bank could become a beach. Whites only. Spiders who are drawn to rising heat populate the ceiling of Jefferson's memorial. Once the sun sets, the temperature drops; they lose their grip and fall. Bodies bounce off my shoulders, bodies land in my hair. Guards call this the *spider rain*.

LINCOLN, MIDNIGHT

Never have I seen such majestic shins. He is pensive, frock coat unbuttoned, larger than once planned, and if he were to stand his head would nearly scrape the ceiling. What if that is Robert E. Lee's face, sculpted into the waves of hair? No telling of the Union without the telling of the Confederacy. No stranger a feat than infusing Alabama marble with paraffin to better let the sky's light in. The sculptor took these hands from a May 1860 cast, before he had signed any proclamations or called 75,000 volunteers to an army. In May 1860, he was only a Republican nominee. Leonard Volk came to Illinois, and as he prepared the plaster he asked Abraham Lincoln for two gestures: one hand a fist, and in the other, something to be held loosely. In the statue this postures openness, conciliation. In reality, Lincoln was holding a broom handle he'd fetched from his tool shed.

CHERRY TREE REBELLION

To save the cherry trees—O Cissy O Eliza O Clara O Catherine—
you buckled your shoes and descended. Fifty of you marched
your petition to the President's house; a flimflam, he called
it, cooked up by the newspapers. The next day, a hundred
and fifty of you marched to the Tidal Basin. You grabbed the
shovels from the Civilian Conservation Corps, refilling holes.
You hitched your skirts and chained yourselves to the trunks.
The Secretary of the Interior sent lunch over, and coffee, cup
after cup, coaxing your bladders toward betrayal. O Cissy O
Eliza O Clara O Catherine, O Valkyries in muslin, I imagine
you staying deep into the night of November 1938. For the
first two hours, you talk. In the third hour, you sing. In the
fifth hour, your stoles come alive: fresh dew on the eyes of each
fox, fur damp, an exhalation that fogs as if breath. But you'd
already gone home to your warm beds. Roosevelt ordered the
graveyard crew to dig fast, and the men did.

ROOSEVELT, MIDNIGHT

The Depression is a crash of water; terraced flow narrates the TVA dam. Carnelian granite erupts to blocks, naked in their etched enjambments: *I hate / war*. A man leans in to his radio. The breadline waits in bronze. Eleanor stands in her resolute suit to address the United Nations. Everywhere, his words. Missing: her words. Missing: Lucy Mercer. Missing: FDR's cigarette, clenched at a rakish angle. For his version of the story, head to 9th Street and Pennsylvania Avenue, NW, and look for a block the size of a desk, with *In Memory of* and the years of his birth and death. That's his version. This version is an amusement park. The memorial opened and, four years later, they added a wheelchair. The stone is beautiful when snow falls. The stone is beautiful when the cherry blossoms accumulate, windswept. This sculpted wall is supposed to speak of WPA, CCC, the alphabet agencies. But its Braille dots are oversized beyond any one fingertip. *This is gibberish*, a visitor says, feeling the spaces between.

EINSTEIN, MIDNIGHT

The memorial's shape is cumulative, clay on clay. His brow wrinkles, his sweater sags, toes flex gently in open sandals. What you see is his 1953 face combined with an imagined body. Mass is the presence of energy, an object's resistance to anything other than what it is already doing. Yes, you may sit on Albert's lap. Look past your feet; those 2,700 studs map what we knew of a particular day's sky. Did you know he patented a refrigerator with no moving parts? His fridge collaborator was the one who asked him to cosign the letter that said, *It may become possible to set up a nuclear chain reaction in a large mass of uranium.* Later, he'd say that if he'd known Germans would fail, he'd have never urged Americans to succeed. When he applied for clearance on the Manhattan Project, our Army refused. Now, an artist works into the dawn hours, looping with her crochet needle until his figure is shrouded in pink, purple, and teal. *Yarn-bombing*, we call this. Anything, in the right hands, can be made to explode.

TITANIC, MIDNIGHT

A dollar toward the cause came from Col. John Jacob Astor's own pocketbook, paid to Mrs. Archibald Forbes. They had settled up after a bridge game on the night of April 14, 1912. His body would eventually be inventoried, as they all were. No. 124, male, about age fifty, light hair and moustache. He wore a blue serge suit and a flannel shirt, "J.J.A." on the collar. He wore brown boots, a belt with gold buckle, diamonds in his cuff links and ring. That's not Astor seen here though, arms thrown wide. Gertrude Vanderbilt Whitney is said to have based the face on her brother, who went down with the *Lusitania*. The figure designed by Whitney is only vaguely sexed, not clothed so much as draped. *Erected by the Women of America*, says the inscription, meaning twenty-five thousand women who mailed in their dollar bills. This is the second installation. Officials disappeared the memorial for thirty years before it reappeared down by Fort McNair, saying, *We need to make way for the Kennedy Center.* The construction was a convenient excuse. There had been miscalculations and, in 1936, an unusual snowmelt. No one could quite shake the memory of the Great Potomac Flood: how waters had lapped the feet, then the knees, waist, the lithe pectorals, before finally crowning his brow.

AMERICAN ROME

Marion "Shepilov" Barry Jr. (1936–2014)

Marionberry: jams of Washington
state. I thought they were mocking this city.
Take a mayor and boil his sugar down—
spoon-spreadable, sweet. We take presidents
and run them in a game's fourth-inning stretch.
We take Bullets and turn them to Sea Dogs.

Remember that vote, that ballot? *Sea Dogs
Dragons Stallions Express.* The Washington
Wizards was no more or less of a stretch.
We wave gavels like wands in this city.
We're the small town in which a president
can plant some roses. Each time I sit down

to try and say goodbye, all I write down
is *Dear City.* My neighbor walks his dogs
past a monument to a president's
terrier, Fala, forever bronzed. Washington
has no J Street, no Z, yet the city
maps attend to fifty states and a stretch

of five blocks NE Metro track—a stretch
named Puerto Rico Avenue. Bow down

to the unmapped names: Chocolate City,
Simple City. Ben serves up chili dogs
through a riot, and Walter Washington
is the first and last time a president

picks our mayor. The truth is, presidents
come and go, four or eight years at a stretch.
Barry said, *I'm yours for life, Washington*;
Emperor Marion, who could get down
with Chuck Brown. Later, reporters will dog
his *Bitch set me up*, his graft. Dear City,

will you let me claim you as my city?
To love you is to defy precedent.
Your quadrants hustle like a pack of dogs
around the hydrant Capitol. They stretch
and paw, they yap and will not settle down.
Traffic: the berry to Washington's jam.

For city miles, Barry's motorcade stretched.
We laid him among vice presidents, down
where the dogs seek congress in Washington.

PIGS IN SPACE

Landing at the Sea of Tranquility,
the clock calls for breakfast—
eight squares of bacon, coated in gelatin;
dehydrated peaches; apricot cereal cubes.

No salt on the loose, no spice,
fifteen cups of coffee per astronaut.

All this fine-tuned in the eight years
since Gemini pilot John Young's pocket
revealed a corned beef sandwich
courtesy Wolfie's of Cocoa Beach,
which he offered to Gus Grissom
as the crumbs broke away and floated
toward the fickle innards of the ship.

Now, everything bound into bar or pouch,
cocktail shrimp hand-selected to squeeze
one by one through the tubing.

Inventing the space taco will take
another two decades. Sturdy tortillas
will be fortified for shelf life,
glued together by creamed onions.

In 2008, Korean scientists will perfect
how to prepare kimchi
without the lactic bacterial fizz
that might, given cosmic rays,
just happen to mutate.

But we are not there yet,
and for days the Apollo 11 menu
has asked them to imagine one paste
as beef, another as chicken;
to discern first tuna, then salmon.

As they ready to step outside
the lunar module, Buzz Aldrin unscrews
a tiny vial drawn from his private pouch,
and the wine drapes at one-sixth gravity.
His fingertips grip a tiny chalice,
while the other hand places
a wafer on his tongue. During all this,

NASA cuts the feed. Soon they'll return
to regularly scheduled acts of faith,
releasing hydrogen and oxygen
to mix inside the fuel cell:

from that, a gathering of water,
and from that, a chowder of corn.

BILOXI BACON

If Marc Chagall's father
had hauled fish in Mississippi
instead of Vitebsk,

in his paintings
holy mullet would
wing over his rooftops—

mullet, on violin—rooster
and mullet, mullet and goat.
In his chapel of mullet-paned glass

we would gather
to watch each fish relay
the baton of its body

from wave to wave,
across a marathon of hunger.
The body, fried, cradled in grits.

Smoked body, lacquered in cane.
We save the gizzard,
the star-white milt,

while bridal roe bursts
with promise of morning.
When casting nets to the Gulf,

who are we to judge grace?
Chagall saw the wonder
of what sustains us: how one

can scavenge the bottom
and still rise, without apology,
by the silvered dozen.

RHYMES WITH

I stop off on Route 301 to debate
between quarter-bushel bags of oranges—
Temples and Ortaniques I'll bring back
to the presser we bought cheap, scrubbed clean.
Wear-Ever, promises the stamped metal.

I have been in lust with Florida's strange:
her match of pastel blue to forest green;
her north more Southern than her south;
how alligators and crocodiles share nine miles
of pond with one shore brackish, the other fresh.

Sporange, promises the dictionary.
Or *Blorenge*, a mountain in southeast Wales.
In moments like this I must pitch my stance
so that I don't fall down the mountain,
into a Welsh valley,

into the river of Usk.
We'll work for an hour, slicing and pressing,
until we've filled two bottles to the brim.
What two bodies couldn't make music,
within such a tight embrace of aluminum?

STILL LIFE WITH SEX

But first, a skull grinning amongst the grapes;
but first, hydrangea moons barely risen;
but first, milky bowls congregating in the sink
and sticky spoons congregating in the bowls;
but first, that vegetal stink; but first,
clank of pipes filling with air; but first,
dirt on your end of the couch; but first,
dirt from your Monday shoes;
but first, a canteen of water;
but first, five lagers;
but first, *Magnum P.I.*;
but first, Tom Selleck; but first,
kiss me because you clutter the pewter;
kiss me because you track in necessary dirt.
Picture a violin, then add prosciutto.
We are trying to make space and hold it open.
The skull that grins amongst grapes grins at us.
But first, those globes of hydrangea;
there they are, perfect, and cratering to our touch.

HAINS POINT

The old men chide each other to tee up quick, before the rain comes. I want to buy a fountain soda, sit on the porch, and eavesdrop. I want to buy a pitcher of beer. I walk the mini-green, swoops of turf and brick that have been here since 1931. The city assembled this spit over a dozen years from nineteenth-century dredgings. My dad detoured our Cadillac along the channel so we'd see *The Awakening*, five pieces that hinted at a giant body breaking ground to breathe. The Peace Garden's funding never came through. The Navy enclosed four acres to build a steel shed, contents unknown, and *The Awakening* moved to Maryland. The sidewalk is swept with mucky silt and I'm getting mosquito-bit, watching ducks toddle and peck. On the far bank, National glimmers. One plane after another insists on liftoff as the storm eases across the river. The old men chide each other, *Go on now*. They give each other answers no man gives when a woman does the asking.

WINTER GARDEN PHOTOGRAPH

After Roland Barthes

Barthes withholds this image from *Camera Lucida*—

Henriette, the five-year-old who grows up to be his mother,
her hands on her hips.
He couldn't bear that our gaze might find her

ordinary,
as one might find this snapshot
of my grandparents arriving in Rapid City, South Dakota.

Her precise handwriting on the back declares
their "America the Beautiful" tour.
Grandma Jean's jaunty scarf, Carl in his crisp white shirt—
1990. In 1991,

I pick up the calendar she kept
by her reading chair. Her neat script fills the square of
January 22:
Carl died. Life is over.

The woman in green jacket and green skirt, full throttle,
smiles toward the camera

as she rounds the corner of the terminal,
purse under one arm and blue carry-on under the other.

Because this photograph is not mine to keep, I take
a photograph of it.

Barthes says I am now operator
and referent,
sliver of thumb and palm visibly cradling Kodak print.

The rest of January 1991 stays blank.

February, blank. March, bare.
But then a church meeting is scheduled.
She pencils in a lunch.
Yes, she will come to the recital.

Her cursive wakens the days.
Even in winter, the garden can call itself to bloom.

CARD TABLE

A practical gift for moving to the city:
good cherry squared around black vinyl,
four long legs that fold within itself
as a greyhound does, disappearing into a nap.
Just big enough for a bridge match
if I'd ever had four people willing to kiss knees.
Just big enough to let me call a corner
of that S Street studio my breakfast nook,
stacked with a week's worth of newspapers
while I ate cereal cross-legged on my futon.
Just big enough to pull out every few years
and complain how small the table was,
too crowded as a desk, too low for my chairs.
In January, we stared at the strange space
wedged between two kitchen doorways.
Might as well try the card table.
We stacked onions there, then potatoes,
then tomatoes and peaches, and it became
the chopping table; stirring table; serving table.
Now, the first morning she is gone,
I see a swipe in the vinyl where a hot dish
burned through, and realize I forgot

to ask for anything—a ring, her sheet music—
so what I have is this reminder
that she, too, was once a girl in a city,
and that she knew I'd always need a table.

IN PRAISE OF PINTOS

Phaseolus vulgaris.
Forgive these mottled punks,
children burst
from the piñata of the New World,
and their ridiculous names
of Lariat, Kodiak, Othello,
Burke, Sierra, Maverick.
Forgive these rapscallions that
would fill the hot tub with ham
while their parents
go away for the weekend,
just to soak in that salt.
Forgive their climbing instinct.
Forgive their ignorance
of their grandparents who
ennobled Rome's greatest:
Fabius, Lentulus, Pisa, Cicero
the chickpea. *Legume*
is the enclosure, fruit in pod,
but *pulse* is the seed.
From the Latin, *puls*
is to beat, to mash, to throb.

Forgive that thirst. Forgive
that gallop. Beans are the promise
of outlasting the coldest season.
They are a wink in the palm of God.

THE VOW

But never for us the flitch of bacon though,
That some may win in Essex at Dunmow.

So promises the old wives' tale,
a covenant according to Chaucer:
that if tomorrow I trek to Dunmow Church
and swear before God and congregation
not a fight, no single quarrel,
in 366 days not even once wishing
to be un-married to you,
that hog is ours for the taking.

My love, what
limp victory that would be,

sweet silence of perfect agreement
as we swing a pork trophy between us,
walking the many miles home—
the fatback won, the battle lost.

I reserve my right to a good spat,
to the meat's spit in flame.

I take joy in choosing you again and again.

LITTLE LOVE POEM

The 6 a.m. sun considers everything,
humming its way past the Capitol.

I reheat yesterday's coffee,
put lima beans into a pot:

Fordhook, always Fordhook,
drizzle of olive oil, pinch of salt, shake

of chili flakes. The chicken broth
comes to boil for a minute

before I cover, simmer. Soon he'll wake,
and I'll ask him to put a record on,

something with no words;
bowls, spoons, a single twist of pepper.

DEATH BY CHOCOLATE

A man wants my take on his novel
where a wife dies with a peanut in her mouth
after we've met her husband, in the act with his secretary
in the passenger seat of a late-life convertible.
A man wants my take on his novel
where the husband's marital issues are solved
by her anaphylactic collapse after he serves her takeout
spiked with a cashew, and for another 300 pages
he wonders, *Was it an accident? Or did I
know?* Somewhere out there a man
is writing a novel about a chef with a taste
for adding shrimp paste to curry and his unsuspecting
shellfish-allergic wife, and I will be asked
for my take on it. I have been offered dozens of takes
on my own death. Suggestions abound.
Death by ice cream. Death by cake. Death by cucumber,
though that would take a while;
perhaps gazpacho as a shortcut. *Death by mango.*
Death by Spanish omelette. Death by dairy,
an abstraction sexy to someone who has never side-eyed
cream brought out slopping toward the coffee;
who has never felt histamine's palm at her throat,
who says *Cheese makes life worth living.*

These wives! I get you, women who
did not grow up aspiring to be a plot device.
We almost die a lot. Or: we die a lot,
almost. We're over it. Our mouths have more to say.

AN ACCOMMODATION

Pistachio's buds of salt-funk;
cayenne macramé of boiled crawfish;

cantaloupe's tacky, thin sugar;
the first time I eat a thing

I can eat anything.
The allergy requires initial exposure

before my mast cells gather,
before my body says *No.*

Let's consider your need to center me
on the table, to call my portion

naked or *plain* while offering
others the "real" version.

Let's examine your suggestion
we put warnings on the cabinets,

attach my name to a list.
First time, I tasted

a kind of kindness. Then
came my second reckoning.

INTERSECTIONALITY

In the diagram, Bob
is a striped blue triangle.
Some people do not like Bob.
Down with stripes.

Down with triangles.
Bob is at the intersection of
stripey-ness and blue-ness,
of triangle-ness and Bob-ness.

Luckily, there are "liberation groups."
Here is where the model
starts to fail me: maybe *liberation*
has come in the form of four taxis,

each waiting to carry Bob away
from this intersection.
*Bob should not have to choose
any one taxi,* I am told.

Or maybe Bob does not
want to go? Bob has noticed
the quality of the bodega's coffee.
Bob likes this intersection.

Bob can get a pretty good deal
on buying a one-bedroom.
Bob is a striped blue triangle.
Bob is a damn gentrifier.

In 1995, I flunked a Driver's Ed quiz
on intersections
because I could not model
how traffic proceeds at a four-way stop.

In my head, each car
arrived at the same time.
What happens when you yield
to the car on your right,

who yields to the car on his right,
who yields to the car on her right,
who yields to you?
No one goes anywhere.

The reality,
my teacher once explained,
is someone always claims
the right of way.

Four allies in four cars
meet at a four-way stop,
you know the one,
it's over by Bob's bodega.

The woman's car on my right yields,
the woman's car on her right yields,
the third car rolls a window down,
then I hear, *Do you mind?*

We're in a hurry
for her OIT appointment.
What I call my disability
you call her disease:

treatable, curable, Thank God.
So that must be your daughter,
in the passenger seat?
She looks just like you.

CUSTOMER SERVICE IS

We take pride in serving the
We're accustomed to servicing the
Please take the attached
Please answer these six
Please answer these eight
This will only be a quick
If microphones don't reach, then
If ramps are required, then
If you need audio, then
If you need visual, then
We request one week's
We request one month's
All reasonable requests will
A flock of surveys is a surveillance.
A stampede of stairs is an architecture.
An expectation of elevators is a favor.
An "oh-crap" of crips is a caucus.
But I have an aunt who is
I had a friend who was
We practice best
We follow the

You have to see our
You have to stand up for
Your help is so
Your answers will be

SAY THE WORD

To be apart, I'm told.
To be asunder.
To be a privative, negative, reversing force.
To be reached only by oaths and curses.
To have black sheep sacrificed in my name
because I'm a god, yes,
as we are all gods on occasion.
To be bodied as I am bodied.
To be rich of earth,
which is to be chronically chthonic.
To be where the gems are—
underground.
To be Dīs. To be Dīs. To be Dīs.
To reject any pickaxe disguised as love.

POP

We call an unpuffed piece
the *old maid*

but she's just the one
who read the fine print.

Germ and sugar curled
in her hard hull,

deciding whether
to shake out her sheets.

Sometimes it's worth it—
pan, oil, flame.

Sometimes you must
hold the steam within you.

SELF-PORTRAIT WITH GEORGE CATLIN

"Generokee": a term describing one who claims
a distant and unsubstantiated relationship
to an American Indian tribe.

If I'd only ever seen one Catlin,
this would be a different conversation:

the rich red and blue oil paint
of *Stu-mick-o-súcks, Buffalo Bull's Back Fat,*
Head Chief, Blood Tribe, which
the Smithsonian catalogs as

Ethnic – Indian – Blackfoot
Dress – ethnic – Indian dress
Recreation – leisure – smoking
Object – other – smoking material

Or the frank gaze and stacked beads
of *Koon-za-ya-me, Female War Eagle*
(Ethnic – Indian – Iowa).
If there was just one on the wall

I might find it my favorite, amidst
a nineteenth-century blur of bucolic takes on
waterfalls and Manifest Destiny
(Landscape – phenomenon – rainbow).

Instead, I rock back and forth
on the museum's mezzanine,

trying to take in Catlin's
Indian Gallery—a grid of faces,
all that specificity of name and tribe
hidden beneath a number,

which I may look up within a replica
of Catlin's own catalog,
as if checking the price on a couch
I've admired off the showroom floor.

What I could have noticed, viewing
the display of "his Indians,"
is how alone each subject is kept,
their only counsel his admiring gaze,

or how portraits share warm, puffy light,
a hint of foliage, making it easy to hide
whether painted on expedition
to the Plains or to London,

where he paid his subjects to dance
for the gallery's crowds.

And yet. *And yet*
what would we have, if we
did not have this? Here
is that "we," cozy

as an infected blanket.
So much taken under the decree
of numbered days,
the promised dwindling of "noble

savages." This occurs to me
not at all in 2002, when
(Ethnic – White – Suburbia)
I buy postcards in the gift shop

from a show I don't enjoy,
but have been told I'm supposed

to enjoy. A push-pin's
worth of heritage, and the claim:

One-thirty-secondth, I think.
Cherokee. Maybe Navajo.

BASS PRO SHOPS

Bass Pro Shops began as a counter for worms and bait in the back of a Brown Derby liquor store in Branson, Missouri. Bass Pro Shops now makes over four billion dollars a year. The one in Memphis contains two restaurants, a hundred-room hotel, and America's tallest freestanding elevator. The one in Harlingen, Texas, has a twelve-lane bowling alley called Uncle Buck's Fishbowl and Grill.

Uncle Buck's BBQ sauce is available in the condiments plaza. There are plazas for grills, tents, sleeping bags, footwear, and thermal-lined jackets. Bass Pro Shops offers reels, rods, and terminal tackle for all of your needs. Bass Pro Shops carries Tracker, SeaCraft, and Kenner for all of your needs. Bass Pro Shops has partnered with Remington, Winchester, and Benelli for all of your needs. The shotguns are upright and gleaming. Perhaps this stuffed menagerie of deer and bear should haunt me, but I'm only tired and a little hungry. Once, at a party in Connecticut, I opened a closet and found two mounted zebra heads tucked to the side behind some coats.

In Bass Pro Shops, fifty cents will get me twenty rounds at the shooting arcade. A shooting arcade is another name for a catch-and-release rifle. I would like to understand the thing that broke in me when someone aimed not a gun at my father, but a whole plane. I can hear the broken thing rattle as I walk.

The secret to enjoying camouflage-colored jellybeans is to ignore how they look in your palm. Uncle Buck's hostess wants to talk Happy Hour specials. The Harlingen Outdoor World has a tank fashioned like a cross-section of a lake. Perch, catfish, and bass the color of dishwater circle and gawp. Bass Pro Shops puts in five entrances and a loading dock and calls it the outdoors. Bass Pro Shops puts a roof on something and calls it a world.

NON-COMMISSIONED: A QUARTET

A Golden Shovel
after Gwendolyn Brooks,
"Gay Chaps at the Bar."

I.

No one chose us. We
chose ourselves. What a man knew
in the concrete embrace of bunkers—how
or who—would never make it to
the foxhole. A sergeant catches the order
as it trickles down his just
commander's leg. We hauled the
water. We led the dash.
We're the vertebras necessary
so the skeleton can dance. We're the
eighteen rounds in the length
of a minute; the fifty pounds of
an M1928 haversack. We're the gayety
of five-card draw in
dead night, the muffled barter of good
smokes for bad booze. Privates taste
fear. A corporal will spit it out. Whether
a man remembers to thread the
diaper of his pack: the stuff of raillery,
except when it should

save your life. We chose to be
grenade men. There was no *slightly.*
There is no plum butter, no bread, no iced
tea, no lemon. There is a meat can, and
there may be meat in it. What's given
to a boy as he trembles, as he turns green,
is the lesson of swim or
goddammitswim. You serve or are served
on a stretcher. Once home, belly up
to the bar and speak of the hot
dusks—how you aimed the mortar—and
remember us, who stayed in the jungles lush.

II.

The difference between liver and
foie gras, we were taught, is in how we
hold a beast's head before feeding. We knew

the throat lining to be beautifully
calloused, like a palm. We learned how
to load the gavage, to

simmer corn in fat to give
their flesh fat in return. They told us to
keep the men. We discarded women

after hatching and the
smell was foul, but so goes summer.
We could almost taste the spread,

rich in iron, surrendering to a tongue the
way an ice cube melts in the tropics.
Nothing was wasted and of

the lies they'll tell, that's the worst: that our
care was a form of waste. It was love.
Everything stings less when

shot with rye. We took time to
pin tin to each swollen breast, to persist
even when they hollered or

the cage held more than it could hold.
We stroked their throats and called it a
sign of hunger

if they swallowed. We took off
shoes that shone with their filth. We knew
their feathers would not stay white.

No one had to give that speech,
nor show us how
their eyes would glaze when ready to

slaughter. How can I make
you understand? This is not a
form of betrayal. Look.

In the field, the officer's job is to make an
office: anything else is an empty omen.

III.

But
nothing
ever
taught
us
to
be
islands.

IV.

If a mother cradles her son's face and
praises how *brave* he is, how *smart*,
how nimble or athletic,
she is teaching him the language
of easy victory—ten points scored for
his team, the test aced, the prick of this
needle to which he did not weep. An hour
in the trench offered what was

a different dictionary. We do not
speak of smart, or brave, or *honor in
battle*. That's for telegrams to the
parents, the posthumous curriculum.
Little sprinter, you have no
advantage in this marathon, no stout
legs to carry you to the finish line's lesson.
Those soldiers who showed
grace with a bayonet understood how
the body must become a weapon to
be wielded; how every chat
is a conversation with

the self we want to save; how death
listens in, nodding. We
laughed at the lieutenants who brought
photos of sweethearts, because no
girl wants to kiss a mouth full of brass.
If the only volume is fortissimo,
it's not music that's playing. Among
every hour, what I recall is our
silences. Our greatest talents—
accomplishing with a look what to
a weaker man required a holler.
We raised them. We laid them down.
We learned faces but not the
names, and we left lording to the lions.
The roof of the house I lived in
had a chevron's peak. I took in this
breath and then there was no other air.

LAZARUS

The cat flops and swims along the carpet,
ecstatic in her clawing, because I am alive,
despite the three days' absence that she took as
my death. She could vomit in sheer joy,
and later she will, but for now
it's head-butts and pantomime of mewing
with her jaw that ached and ran dry of sound
after my first night gone. Though I know
each of us would be better off
if she did not care quite so much, if
she displayed the feline diffidence promised—
water, kibble, company, she'll be fine—
I confess to delighting in this small miracle
I perform in her eyes, this
resurrection. After a brief pause
to lovingly tend to her own asshole,
the cat resumes her yawp and purr.
Could I learn to greet the world this way,
to take nothing for granted? First
I'd have to think you all had died, of course,
but death would be temporary.
Truth is, I've tried odder routes to ecstasy.

EPIC

After C. P. Cavafy's "Ithaka"

As I set out for home—
back home to my apartment,
to my vengeful cat, back home
to a betrothed who never
was one for textile arts—

I hope the voyage is a long one.
I hope that Homer finds me
on my great journey,
on a bar stool in Ocala
one March Sunday at noon,

though it occurs to me
after I am served
the bowl of boiled peanuts
that my hunger in this moment,

is not heroic. Who am I
in these stories? One by one
I shell those soft bodies,
warm against my bottom teeth,
tipping meat into my mouth.

Did they, too, once have names?
Did they once have sons?

How silly they look, in their little boat
with its checkered placemat sail.
I take a swig of a Bloody Mary,
spiked with ocean and jalapeño,
the one eye of my forehead pulsing.

I will get back in the car.
I will drive another 800 miles
with Aeolus's bagged breath
stashed in my glove compartment.

And if I find home poor, home
won't have fooled me, I
who have forged a life
that consists of leaving my life.

I'll recall I once sat at a bar
wiping Cajun broth from my chin
with a twelfth cocktail napkin.

Blame Nobody, I sang,
Nobody—
Nobody—
Nobody did this to me.

Acknowledgments

Poems previously appeared, often in earlier versions, in *Agni*, *The Arkansas International*, *Bennington Review*, *Birmingham Poetry Review*, *Cherry Tree: A National Literary Journal*, *Copper Nickel*, *Gravy*, *The Mackinac*, the *Nation*, the *New York Times*, *Oxford American*, *Poetry International*, *Salamander*, *The South Carolina Review*, *Southern Indiana Review*, *SWWIM Every Day*, and *Waxwing*.

"The Sniper Dance," "Weak Ocean," and "Bass Pro Shops" won the Adult Poetry Category of the 33rd Annual Larry Neal Writers' Awards (2016), administered by the D.C. Commission on the Arts and Humanities. "Non-Commissioned: A Quartet" won the 2015 C. P. Cavafy Poetry Prize from *Poetry International*.

"Elephant," "Hains Point," and "The Sniper Dance" appear in *Written in Arlington*, edited by Katherine E. Young (Paycock Press, 2020). "Still Life with Sex" appears in *Still Life with Poem: Contemporary Natures Mortes in Verse*, edited by Jehanne Dubrow and Lindsay Lusby (Literary House Press, 2016). "Non-Commissioned: A Quartet" appears in *The Golden Shovel Anthology: New Poems Honoring Gwendolyn Brooks*, edited by Peter Kahn, Ravi Shankar, and Patricia Smith (University of Arkansas Press, 2017). "Kiss Me" appears in *Women of Resistance: Poems for a New Feminism*, edited by Danielle Barnhart and Iris Mahan (OR Books, 2018). "Jefferson, Midnight" appears in *The Eloquent Poem*, edited by Elise Paschen (Persea Books, 2019). "My Whitenesses" appears in *We Hold America: Poetry from the New Labor Movement*, edited by Rebecca Gayle Howell and Ashley M. Jones (University Press of Kentucky, forthcoming 2022).

"The Conversation" was commissioned by the Academy of American Poets in October 2014 to celebrate National Archives Month, and "Say the Word" was featured in Poem-a-Day, January 2020; along with "American Rome," these poems are archived at Poets.org. "Weak Ocean" was featured as Kore Press's Poem of the Week in 2016. "Death by Chocolate" was featured in "We Will Not Be Exorcised," a *New York Times* Opinion portfolio on disability in June 2019, edited by Jillian Weise and Khadijah Queen. "Customer Service Is" was featured as Split This Rock's Poem of the Week in April 2018, received a "Best of the Net" nomination, and is archived in the Quarry online database; it also appears tandem to "Roundtable Discussion on Poetics and Disability," presented by *Poetry International* in May 2018.

*　*　*

My thanks to the team at W. W. Norton, including Jill Bialosky and Drew Weitman. I am grateful to early readers including HL, MT, GB, JC, AS, EM, BFDB, KD, DAM, AH, CG, NEI, ELR, and members of the D.C.-area poetry community. Support for writing this collection came from the Munster Literature Centre, the Hermitage Artist Retreat, Virginia Center for the Creative Arts, and the D.C. Commission on the Arts and Humanities, as well as in the form of camaraderie with the University of Tampa Low-Residency Master of Fine Arts in Creative Writing Program, the Southern Foodways Alliance, and the Disabled & D/deaf Writers Caucus. My love to my family (Beasleys and Pruetts), to the Taylors and Waechters, and particularly to Champneys Taylor.